Oceans

Surviving in the Deep Sea

by Michael Sandler

Consultant: Daniel H. Franck, Ph.D.

PUBLISHING COMPANY, INC.

New York, New York

CREDITS

Cover, Al Giddings; Title page, Al Giddings; 4, Courtesy of NOAA; 5, Denis Scott/Corbis; 6, Steve Stankiewitz; 7, Photodisc/Getty Images; 9, Courtesy of NOAA; 10(t), Peter Batson/Explore the Abyss.Com Limited; 10(b), Lawson Wood/Corbis; 11, Robert Hubeman/SuperStock; 12, Rubberball/SuperStock; 13, Courtesy of NOAA; 14, Al Giddings; 15, Al Giddings; 16, Courtesy of DOER Inc. (Deep Ocean Exploration and Research); 17, Courtesy of NOAA; 18, Al Giddings; 19, Al Giddings; 20, Al Giddings; 21(t), Peter Herring/Image Quest Marine; 21(b), Peter Batson/Explore the Abyss.Com Limited; 22, Courtesy of NOAA; 23, Courtesy of NOAA; 24, Alexis Rosenfeld/Science Photo Library/Photo Researchers, Inc.; 25(t), AFP/Getty Images; 25(b), Alexis Rosenfeld/Science Photo Library/Photo Researchers, Inc.; 26–27, Macduff Everton/Corbis.

EDITORIAL DEVELOPMENT by Judy Nayer
DESIGN AND PRODUCTION by Paula Jo Smith

Library of Congress Cataloging-in-Publication Data

Sandler, Michael.
  Oceans : surviving in the deep sea / by Michael Sandler.
    p. cm. — (X-treme places)
  Includes bibliographical references (p.   ) and index.
  ISBN 1-59716-087-3 (lib. bdg.)— ISBN 1-59716-124-1 (pbk.)
1. Underwater exploration—Juvenile literature. 2. Deep diving—Juvenile literature. 3. Earle, Sylvia A., 1935—Juvenile literature. I. Title. II. Series.

  GC65.S262 2006
  551.46—dc22

                    2005008962

For more information, write to Bearport Publishing Company, Inc., 101 Fifth Avenue, Suite 6R, New York, New York 10003. Printed in the United States of America.

1 2 3 4 5 6 7 8 9 10

Contents

Into the Twilight Zone

Through the helmet of her suit, Dr. Sylvia A. Earle stared down into the water. She was about to make the deepest **solo** dive in human history. Nothing would connect her to the surface. There would be no lifeline.

Sylvia was diving into a part of the deep sea called the twilight zone. It is a place where the sun's light barely reaches.

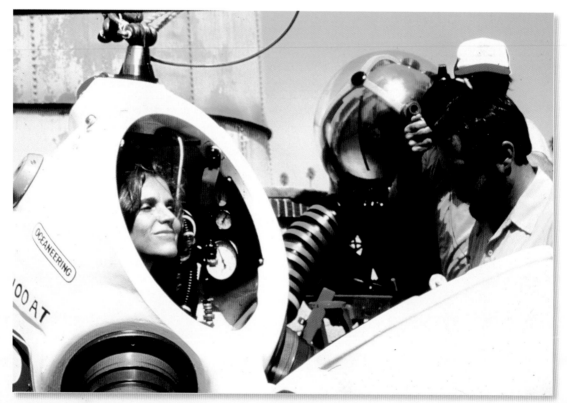

Dr. Sylvia Earle prepares for a deep-sea dive.

When Sylvia told other scientists of her plan, some thought she was crazy. If her life-support systems failed, she would die.

Sylvia entered the water. She headed into the mysterious darkness. If she survived, she would make history.

Ninety percent of all ocean water is below 660 feet (201 m). This water makes up the region known as the deep sea.

Hammerhead sharks can survive in deep ocean waters.

What Are Oceans?

Oceans are the large bodies of salt water that cover Earth's surface. Even though they have different names, all of the world's oceans are connected. Water flows between them, passing from one to another. Together, oceans cover over two-thirds of Earth's surface.

OCEANS OF THE WORLD

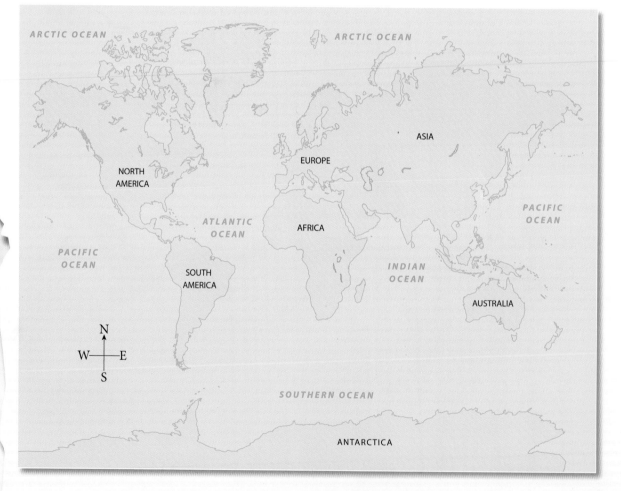

Sylvia was about to dive into the Pacific Ocean. The largest of the world's oceans, the Pacific holds about half of all the water on Earth.

The Pacific is also the deepest ocean. It has an average depth of about 14,000 feet (4,267 m).

Oceans contain 97 percent of all the water on Earth.

Five oceans surround Earth's seven continents, or large masses of land.

What Is the Deep Sea?

Ocean **environments** change the deeper you go into them. Near the surface, the waters are bright, lit up and warmed by the rays of the sun. The light allows **algae** to make food. The algae, in turn, provides food for fish. The environment is filled with life.

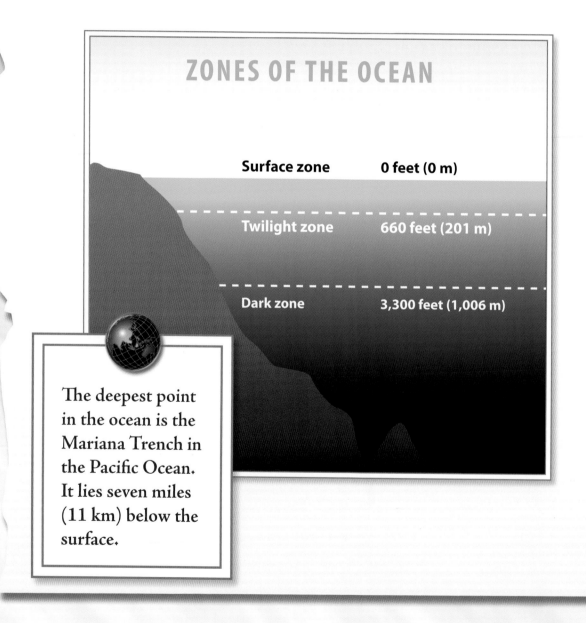

ZONES OF THE OCEAN

Surface zone	0 feet (0 m)
Twilight zone	660 feet (201 m)
Dark zone	3,300 feet (1,006 m)

The deepest point in the ocean is the Mariana Trench in the Pacific Ocean. It lies seven miles (11 km) below the surface.

Farther down, the deep sea begins. The environment becomes more extreme. Less light reaches the deep waters, which are dark and cold. The area between about 660 and 3,300 feet (201—1,006 m) below the surface is called the twilight zone.

From here to the ocean floor, there is no light at all. The water is pitch-black. This region is called the dark zone.

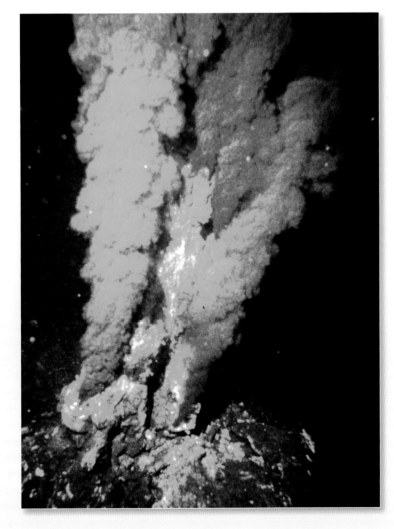

While deep-sea water is usually cold, parts of the ocean have hydrothermal vents. These vents are deep-sea springs that gush out extremely hot water.

Life in the Deep Sea

Although the deep sea gets little light, it is still full of life. It is alive with strange creatures that are specially **adapted** to the extreme environment.

To survive in total darkness, many creatures are bioluminescent (*bye*-oh-*loo*-muh-NESS-uhnt). They have glowing, twinkling lights, created by chemicals in their bodies. These lights can help them to attract **prey** or scare away **predators**.

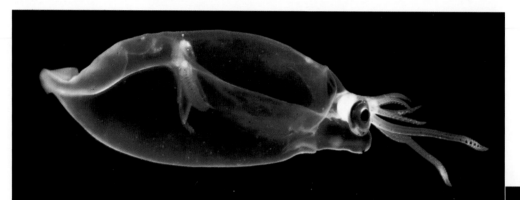

The deep-sea glass squid is almost completely transparent, or see-through.

Giant tube worms are found only on the deep-sea ocean floor.

Many creatures are made up mainly of water. This feature helps them survive in the extreme water **pressure**. Water is heavier than air. In the deep sea, water's weight presses down 100 times greater than it does at the surface.

Jellyfish are 95 percent water, which helps them survive in the deep sea.

Scientists think that three-fourths of all deep-sea creatures are bioluminescent.

Exploring the Deep

People have always been interested in exploring the ocean's depths. The problem is how to survive. How can a person breathe where there is no air? How can a person withstand the crushing water pressure?

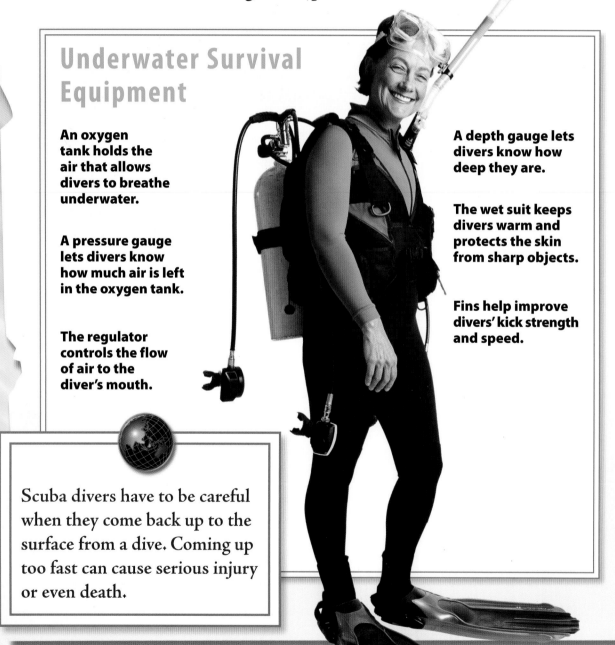

Underwater Survival Equipment

An oxygen tank holds the air that allows divers to breathe underwater.

A pressure gauge lets divers know how much air is left in the oxygen tank.

The regulator controls the flow of air to the diver's mouth.

A depth gauge lets divers know how deep they are.

The wet suit keeps divers warm and protects the skin from sharp objects.

Fins help improve divers' kick strength and speed.

Scuba divers have to be careful when they come back up to the surface from a dive. Coming up too fast can cause serious injury or even death.

At first, divers breathed air that was pumped down from the surface in tubes. Later, **scuba** gear allowed divers to carry their own air supplies in tanks. Scuba divers rarely go down more than 200 feet (61 m), though. The water pressure is too great.

Submarines are built to dive deeper, down to 1,000 feet (305 m). Below these depths, **submersibles** are needed for deep-sea exploration.

Submersible

Viewing lamps light up the pitch-black ocean floor.

Strong metal walls and thick plastic windows protect passengers from crushing deep-sea water pressure.

Cameras let scientists take photos and videos.

Life-support systems provide air for passengers.

Robot arms pick up objects and collect samples.

A Love for the Sea

How did Sylvia become interested in exploring the sea? It began with a family vacation to the New Jersey shore.

"On my first visit . . . a great wave knocked me off my feet," she remembers. Sylvia was thrilled, not scared. She stood up and waited for the next wave.

Marine biologists study life in the sea. Sylvia was one of the first female marine biologists to explore the ocean using scuba equipment.

When Sylvia was 12 years old, her family moved to Florida. Now the ocean lay right in her backyard. About five years later, Sylvia got a chance to try scuba. It was love at first dive.

Sylvia decided she wanted to spend her life exploring the sea. She went to college and became a marine biologist.

Sylvia and dolphin

Living Underwater

Sylvia spent as many hours underwater as she could. In 1970, she got a chance to stay there for a long period of time.

Sylvia was named team leader of a special group of women scientists. Her team would spend two weeks in an underwater **laboratory**, the *Tektite II*, in the Caribbean Sea.

The *Tektite II* was 60 feet (18 m) below the water's surface.

The *Tektite II* had everything the scientists needed to survive: food, water, and most important, oxygen. Using the lab as a base, the women used scuba equipment to explore life in a **coral reef**.

Sylvia studied the fish, how they behaved, and what they ate. For Sylvia, life underwater was a dream come true.

Sylvia Earle and four other **aquanauts** were the first team of women to live beneath the ocean's surface.

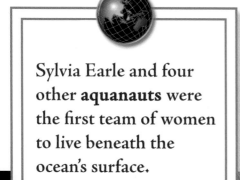

Sylvia shows an underwater find to a teammate.

The Deepest Dive

Sylvia wanted to explore even deeper. In 1979, she prepared to go farther down than any diver had gone before. She was headed 1,250 feet (381 m) below the surface.

To survive at that depth, Sylvia was going to wear a JIM suit. This 1,000-pound (454-kg) metal suit would protect her from the water pressure. It would supply air to breathe. It would protect her against the freezing cold.

Sylvia would attempt her dive in the waters of the Pacific Ocean near the Hawaiian island of Oahu (oh-AH-hoo).

The suit would be **cabled** to the *Star II*, a tiny submarine. The *Star II* would take Sylvia to the ocean floor and then pull her back up.

Still, the sub couldn't help Sylvia if the suit **malfunctioned**. She would die in minutes.

Sylvia in the JIM suit

The JIM suit was named after the first person to wear one, a diver named Jim Jarrett.

Down, Down, Down!

The *Star II* began its dive. Sylvia stood on a small platform in front of the sub, ready for the dive of her life. The sub went down—lower and lower. Then came a bump. The sub had hit bottom—1,250 feet (381 m) down!

Sylvia spent two-and-a-half hours exploring the ocean floor. She holds the world record for the deepest dive outside a submarine.

Sylvia stepped onto the ocean floor. Walking wasn't easy in the heavy, metal suit. The sub beamed a light into the darkness. The sights were amazing! There were red crabs, shimmering lantern fish, and sharks with glowing green eyes! When the time to head up arrived, Sylvia didn't want to leave.

Lantern fish

Hatchet fish

Lantern fish and hatchet fish were two of the strange creatures Sylvia saw on the ocean floor.

The *Deep Rover*

Sylvia had gone as far as anyone could go in a JIM suit. After the dive, she wondered: How could you go even deeper?

Sylvia wanted a small submersible with huge windows and robot arms. She wanted a vehicle that could go 2,000 feet (610 m) deep or beyond. The trouble was, no such vehicle existed.

The *Deep Rover* is completely transparent.
Nothing blocked Sylvia's views.

Sylvia decided to build one! She started a company with Graham Hawkes, a British **engineer**. The two began designing Sylvia's dream machine.

In 1984, the *Deep Rover* was ready. Soon after, in cold Pacific waters off California's coast, Sylvia took the *Deep Rover* 3,000 feet (914 m) down! No solo diver had ever gone so deep.

The *Deep Rover* is shaped like a sphere, or round ball. This shape handles the crushing water pressure better than other designs.

Will the Oceans Survive?

Sylvia was amazed by the sea life she saw from the *Deep Rover*. However, one sight disturbed her. It was shimmering on the ocean floor, shiny and red. It wasn't a fish. It was a soda can. It reminded Sylvia of the dangers that oceans face.

Scuba divers collect garbage from the Mediterranean Sea.

Tankers carry oil across the ocean. If they sink, or leak, oil spills can pollute the seas and destroy marine life.

The oceans are at risk because of what people put into them. Oceans have been used as dumping grounds for garbage and **toxic** chemicals.

The oceans are also at risk because of what people take out of them. People love to eat seafood. Yet, overfishing has driven many sea creatures close to **extinction**.

Thousands of birds and animals died when an oil tanker broke up off the coast of Spain in 2002.

Plastic bags look like food to many sea animals, such as this jellyfish (right).

Working to Save the Sea

Today, Sylvia is still diving and exploring the deep sea. Much of it is unknown territory, like outer space.

"We know more about Mars than we do about the ocean," says Sylvia.

According to scientists, 99 percent of the deep sea has yet to be explored.

A lot of Sylvia's time, however, is spent writing and teaching about oceans. She wants people to know why it is important to protect them. Since so much of Earth is water, the planet's future is connected to the health of the seas.

"If the sea is sick, we'll feel it," says Sylvia. "If it dies, we die. Our future and the state of the oceans are one."

Sylvia Earle in 1998

Just the Facts

MORE ABOUT OCEANS, SYLVIA EARLE, AND DEEP SEA EXPLORATION

- Earth is the only planet in the solar system with bodies of liquid water!

- Sylvia is sometimes called "Her Deepness" because she has spent so much time underwater. She has gone on at least 50 diving expeditions and logged over 6,000 hours under the sea. That amount of time adds up to about 250 days of her life!

- The deepest-diving mammal isn't a human. It's the great sperm whale. It can dive 6,000 feet (1,829 m) down, possibly even deeper! The sperm whale has lungs, not gills like a fish. It can hold its breath for up to two hours.

- Modern scuba equipment was invented by French divers Jacques Cousteau (coo-STOE) and Emile Gagnan in 1943.

Timeline

This timeline shows important events in Sylvia Earle's life and career.

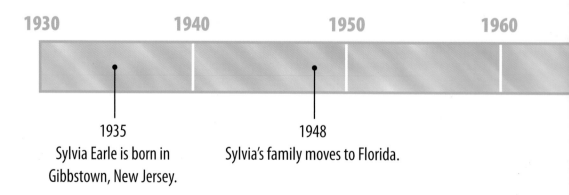

1930   1940   1950   1960

1935
Sylvia Earle is born in
Gibbstown, New Jersey.

1948
Sylvia's family moves to Florida.

- One of the most important early deep-sea vehicles was the bathysphere. This vessel was a 4,500-pound (2,041-kg) hollow steel ball built in 1930. The bathysphere couldn't move on its own. It was suspended by a cable from a boat at the surface.

- *Alvin* is one of the most famous deep-sea exploration vehicles. This submersible makes over 150 dives a year. *Alvin* can dive to 15,000 feet (4,572 m) and carry up to three people.

- In 1960, Jacques Piccard and Don Walsh reached the bottom of the Mariana Trench in a deep-diving vehicle called the *Trieste*. The vessel was huge, but the men were confined to a small protective steel capsule. It took five hours to reach the bottom. Through a tiny window, Piccard and Walsh were able to see a few fish. Today, they are still the only people ever to have seen the deepest place in the sea.

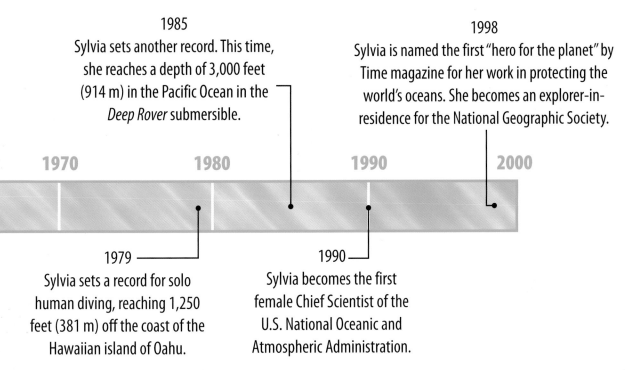

1985
Sylvia sets another record. This time, she reaches a depth of 3,000 feet (914 m) in the Pacific Ocean in the *Deep Rover* submersible.

1998
Sylvia is named the first "hero for the planet" by Time magazine for her work in protecting the world's oceans. She becomes an explorer-in-residence for the National Geographic Society.

1970   1980   1990   2000

1979 —
Sylvia sets a record for solo human diving, reaching 1,250 feet (381 m) off the coast of the Hawaiian island of Oahu.

1990 —
Sylvia becomes the first female Chief Scientist of the U.S. National Oceanic and Atmospheric Administration.

GLOSSARY

adapted (uh-DAP-tid) changed to survive in the environment

algae (AL-gee) a kind of plant that survives mainly in the water and makes food using energy from the sun.

aquanauts (AK-wuh-*nahts*) people who live, explore, and work in undersea environments

cabled (KAY-buhld) attached or connected by a cable, or thick wire or rope

coral reef (KOR-uhl REEF) an ocean habitat created by sea animals called coral that are usually found in shallow tropical waters

engineer (en-juh-NIHR) a person trained to design and build machines, vehicles, roads, or other structures

environments (en-VYE-ruhn-muhnts) types of natural places

extinction (ek-STINGK-shun) when a type of animal or plant dies out

laboratory (LAB-ruh-*tor*-ee) a place used by scientists to conduct experiments

malfunctioned (mal-FUHNGK-shuhnd) stopped working properly

predators (PRED-uh-turz) animals that hunt other animals

pressure (PRESH-ur) the force produced by pressing on something

prey (PRAY) animals that are hunted by other animals

scuba (SKOO-buh) diving equipment that lets a person breathe under the water; scuba stands for Self-Contained Underwater Breathing Apparatus

solo (SOH-loh) done alone

submarines (SUHB-muh-reenz or *suhb*-muh-REENZ) ocean ships that can travel on or below the water's surface

submersibles (suhb-MER-si-bulz) special vehicles designed for deep-sea exploration

toxic (TOK-sik) poisonous

BIBLIOGRAPHY

Baker, Beth. *Sylvia Earle: Guardian of the Sea.* Minneapolis, MN: Lerner Publications (2000).

Byatt, Andrew, Alastair Fothergill, and Martha Holmes. *The Blue Planet: Seas of Life.* New York: DK Publishing (2002).

Conley, Andrea. *Window on the Deep: The Adventures of Underwater Explorer Sylvia Earle.* New York: Franklin Watts (1991).

Earle, Sylvia A. *Dive! My Adventures in the Deep Frontier.* Washington, D.C.: National Geographic Society (1999).

Polking, Kirk. *Oceanographers and Explorers of the Sea.* Springfield, NJ: Enslow Publishers (1999).

READ MORE

Collard III, Sneed B. *The Deep-Sea Floor.* Watertown, MA: Charlesbridge Publishing (2003).

Gowell, Elizabeth Tayntor. *Life in the Deep Sea.* New York: Franklin Watts (1999).

Hall, Kirsten. *Deep Sea Adventures: A Chapter Book.* New York: Children's Press (2003).

McElroy, Lisa Tucker. *Meet My Grandmother: She's a Deep-Sea Explorer.* Brookfield, CT: Millbrook Press (2000).

Simon, Seymour. *Oceans.* New York: HarperTrophy (1997).

LEARN MORE ONLINE

Visit these Web sites to learn more about the deep sea:

seawifs.gsfc.nasa.gov/OCEAN_PLANET/HTML/oceanography_flyby.html

www.ocean.udel.edu/deepsea/home/home.html

www.pbs.org/wgbh/nova/abyss/mission/

www.uncwil.edu/nurc/aquarius

INDEX

ABOUT THE AUTHOR

Michael Sandler lives in Brooklyn, New York, with his family. He has written many books for children and young adults. An avid snorkler and scuba diver, his favorite ocean experience was a week-long exploration of the coral reefs of Palawan, in the Philippines.